Calle Florista

PHOENIX POETS

CONNIE VOISINE

Jan2020

Calle Florista

THE UNIVERSITY OF CHICAGO PRESS

Chicago & London

CONNIE VOISINE is associate professor of English at New Mexico
State University. She is the author of two previous books of poems: *Rare
High Meadow of Which I Might Dream*, also published by the University
of Chicago Press; and *Cathedral of the North*. She lives in Las Cruces,
New Mexico.

The University of Chicago Press, Chicago 60637
The University of Chicago Press, Ltd., London
© 2015 by The University of Chicago
All rights reserved. Published 2015.
Printed in the United States of America

24 23 22 21 20 19 18 17 16 15   1 2 3 4 5

ISBN-13: 978-0-226-29532-9 (paper)
ISBN-13: 978-0-226-29546-6 (e-book)
DOI: 10.7208/chicago/9780226295466.001.0001

Library of Congress Cataloging-in-Publication Data
Voisine, Connie, author.
    Calle Florista / Connie Voisine.
        pages ; cm. — (Phoenix Poets)
    Includes bibliographical references.
    Poems.
        ISBN 978-0-226-29546-6 (ebook) — ISBN 978-0-226-29532-9
(pbk. : alk. paper)
    I. Title.
    PS3622.O37C35 2015
    811'.6—dc23

                                        2014048490

♾ This paper meets the requirements of ANSI/NISO Z39.48-1992
(Permanence of Paper).

for Alma

Oh oh. Too much. Too much. Even now, surmise …

Gwendolyn Brooks

CONTENTS

ACKNOWLEDGMENTS

Grateful acknowledgment is due to the editors of the following magazines and journals in which some of these poems first appeared:

AGNI: "RIP"
The Bloomsbury Review: "Annunciation"
Connecticut Review: "To the Crickets Which Sing in Unison"
Fairy Tale Review: "Ubi sunt qui ante nos fuerunt?" (as "Ubi Sunt")
Flyway: "What is True is You're Not Here"
Hunger Mountain: "New World," "Prayer of the St. of the Hottest Night in Las Cruces," "Calle Florista," and "Psalm to Whoever is Responsible"
The Journal: "Gravid" (as "Sonogram") and "The Self After Modernism"
Northwest Review: "Spanish Language in Mexico, 1993" (as "Spanish Language School")
Passages North: "After the First Road"
Poetry: "The Altar by George Herbert" and "Testament"
Pool: "Unfinished Letter to Death," "Ambidextrous," and "The Internal State of Texas"
Smartish Pace: "Say Uncle," "Two Years in That City," and "I admit that I believe ideas exist regardless"
The White Review: "After" (as "Testament")

"We Are Crossing Soon," "Testament," "Once," and "Ambidextrous" appeared in the anthology *Hick Poetics*, ed. Shelly Taylor and Abraham Smith (Lost Roads Press, 2015).

Also, thanks to my colleagues Sheila Black, Robert Boswell, Karen Brennan, Bobby Byrd, James McMichael, Carol Muske, Antonya Nelson, Jacqueline Osherow, Patty Seyburn, Joe Somoza, and the writers in the Warren Wilson MFA program. Thanks to the University of Chicago Press for publishing poetry (mine included), New Mexico State University for the time, the Fulbright Commission for the means, and the Seamus Heaney Centre and Queen's University in Belfast, Northern Ireland, for another home. Finally, thanks to my husband Rus Bradburd for his love and for keeping us all cheerful.

Calle Florista

CALLE FLORISTA

Don't you remember
our little house on Calle Florista,
the calle with lots of flowers?
There weren't flowers so much as
cats, at least a hundred, lounging in the neighbor's yard
while the bushes roiled with kittens.

They weren't kittens so much as
pecan trees and weeds of the nightshade family,
unwatered except on irrigation days
when the whole neighborhood stood up to its knees in water.

And the water was not water so much as
gravel, and the Calle was not a street, but more
a bunch of rocks lined up in a particular way.
And the "Florista" started last year. The maps
still say Iris Lane.

There were no irises so much as one fat Shar-Pei,
the guard dog to Chinese kings, said the uncle next door
as Sassy yowled in the yard.
Sassy was not a guard dog so much as
not very smart,
though Tio was kind of kingly
sitting in his minivan with a Keystone Light.

What did I do all day?
The boy hit my car with a stick.
His sister stood in the plastic swimming pool.
When would the pecans drop? Tio was waiting.

It wasn't so much waiting as the kids and Tio
worrying about the occasional helicopter
battering by
and the dog and the cats, who were not cats at all
maybe.
And me in that little house, writing about
our street, which changed every day

subtly and in complicated ways.
But for you it was most different—
you were the one who didn't exist,
except as someone
who did not live on Calle Florista.

AS WELL AS YOU CAN

Every morning my feet, deaf and dumb,
gird themselves, provide.
They take me to the river
and back regardless of the world
and its current condition,
my pain, etc.

Is the sky pink?
Who knows? Is there any way around
the symbolic? Silence.
Is that edible? Hmm?

But what about living in darkness,
as they so calmly do?
What about the lumpen sadness of all shoes?
And all day that gravel of socket and bone,
that heel like an adze?

They are not like you or me.
Their cheerfulness
is a miracle: run, stub, trip,
skip the last step, scratch again
under blankets at night.

THE INTERNAL STATE OF TEXAS

This much is known:
It's large and largely dry.
It's been called terrarium-like by experts.
At first, I felt it slowly growing
the requisite cactus and coast.
I wrote letters to the president,
but he vacationed inside me for months at a time.
I can't say Galveston was anything
other than sweet heat and water,
though Dallas was a bitch until I passed it.
It was the fighter jets that got better and better.
They came to appreciate me, too.
In those fabulous formations they swooned
curlicues on those bluest skies,
burning elaborate fuels like there was no tomorrow.
"Dear President,
the streets of downtown
are quite dirty and packed with people
vagrantly wandering."
He was photographed
inside me, with chainsaw,
concerned about longhorns.
I wanted something
even though the dollar stores simmered
like hens on their nests of cleaning supplies,
spatulas, and hair ties.

"Dear President,
I had wanted something, I don't know,
prettier for myself by this age.
Please advise."
Meanwhile, men unscrolled miles
of Scotchgarded fencing.
Esequiel Hernández was actually shot
herding goats, and Krispy Kremes
blindsided everyone. But I was younger then,
before the daring, handsome surgeon
who wore cowboy boots,
before the long convalescence
and all that doctorly handholding.

WE ARE CROSSING SOON

It was hot. We wandered on the pavement.
We knew that soon we would get there.

We thought we were prepared—one says goodbye
and looks for a knife and a proper comb,

and while doing so avoids a crying person.
Soon we would get there, or not soon, but

we would, the bridge not too crowded, the agents
distracted, and the water would not be too wet.

The desert weeping manna in the cool morning will provide.
The streets of El Paso will provide.

We surfed on the ocean and kissed blond girls named Melissa
with each other, astride the dumpsters

behind the TV factory. We were not smooth,
and we wouldn't like living alone, wondering what our

mothers were doing at that moment. At that moment
our mothers were sewing small pieces of old clothes.

Certainly we would arrive the way birds arrive, not through
maps and memory, but some other dark

knowledge, though we knew some would drop
dead from the sky. We had cousins. We smoked cigarettes

whenever we could and the avenues yawned, flustered
with feet—it was so hot—and beyond lay the river

in its cement trough, the highway, the fields
of onions. We shined your shoes with a vigor

unexplained by democracy, our boots crooked
but shining, then your shoes were shining,

spotless down the dusty streets, the quarters
in our hands were shining like a teakettle we would own.

RULES FOR DROUGHT

Don't worry about which fork—
the river is too sandy for dining.

The dust will never behave.

We ask you to refrain from bathing at peak hours.

Try this prickly pear. It helps.

Don't forget the spine of a cactus
comes from a special place
called the areole.

Sink into our particular kind of battle,
which is composed simply of waiting.

Tell time by the change in pitch
of painful light, or the depth of
heat's unbearableness.

Lucky is for the other people.

Bats, which we store by the cloudful,
are the only mammals that fly.

WHAT IS TRUE IS YOU'RE NOT HERE

I lie beneath the stars
and think of you
while the imperious night
rearranges the birds.
But it's dangerous business,
all this personifying.
The night doesn't need
that kind of help,
and the birds are insulted
by my presumptions.

I wonder what you are doing
right now. Over there
it's so different, with grass and rain
and rocks that have learned
to speak in a language we understand.
Boots, they say,
or *eternal*.
On a rainy day,
you might do something quiet—
eat some dinner
then go to bed.

Here in the desert
I find myself counting the warts
on a moon so bright I could read

my watch if I had one, and soon
I'm telling that old fart
the prickly pear lurking near my foot
Knock it off. Don't even try.
Week after week
gnarling up by the patio—
I can only imagine what he's up to.

What's true is what's in front of me:
headlights across the wall of oleanders,
the roadside cross
adorned with plastic flowers
to remind the world someone loved has died.
The truth is the birds are not angry and
the cactus doesn't want to touch me.
The moon is made only of moon.
The patio can shrug its loneliness off,

or rather, the patio is just
cement-colored cement
with dirt on every side.

SAY UNCLE

What's the word for *suffer*?
It's somewhere

between *curbside* and *truculent*
in the humid entries of the

city, between *metal rails,*
dirt shoulder, bleached stones.

The sun is high should be easy,
ask the Wells Fargo building,

and *trees have grown sore*
might be behind the nursing home.

Where would one find *narrow*?
without? *to mourn*? It's not

golf course or *velvet painting.*
It's somewhere else, near

immobile and *shorn,*
which have been rescheduled due to

rain. How would you find *vigil*
and *beautiful mouth*, those two

last seen by the side of the highway.
Can anybody tell me the word

for *sacrifice* is near? What about *love*
and the twins *every morning* and

rocks under my feet?

NEW WORLD

Here the minimalist sky.
Here antelope (pronghorns) and the burnt, high-plains grasses
bound to the edge of the compound, the edge of town,
the edge of, the edge of.
Here glints polish the air to gold.
The antelopes and the few stunted trees
dream about Jonah in the belly of the sky.
Let's have nothing
but gold—it's so pleasing.

One night a man took out an accordion.
So loud, the instrument in this night, and so many
romantic waltzes that I wept just
outside the fire's circle of light.

I knew a lot, once.
Wasn't Naturalism about to happen?
And really, the French and the English,
why should they quit—a battle here, one there,
and their navies refulgent?
And that man, saying such things:
"the night is the very experience of the *there is.*"
Once I knew
that pastries could have a thousand leaves.
The bishop wore a fabulous hat,

and forks and knives
were polished monthly to meditate
in their velvet boxes.

Here the sky represents nothing
but blue, and we go along
inventing new ways of dying:
by the cutting off of hands,
of hair, death by one dirty blanket, and
death by walking.
Death by six pine nuts, by bloody
sunset, by obscure mirage.

I ADMIT THAT I BELIEVE IDEAS EXIST REGARDLESS

Why worry about it?
Any idea has at least one limb that will whip a soul
into a factory of feeling,
where passion becomes clearer,

like a beautiful television
being made right now inside the factory.
It's hard to separate from feeling.
Maybe the soul isn't a fussy eater—
still, it is ravenous

and expensive, like a defensive lineman.
A hammer is only as strong as the hand
who finds it, and God is pure idea

when it comes to football.
Weary, God puts passion in the toolbox
so the lineman can work the world

into one big factory. Watch how the soul
turns on the TV and everything gives in
to formations.

ANNUNCIATION

Was it on Market Street? George Street? Or on the plain grid where
your house is now?
The book's perfume lifted as you touched it: must, dead clover,
wood smoke.
Your flesh became silk, limpid, luminous.
You say nothing about it
but the airport speaks for you—
a whoosh that shakes the fruit trees, clotheslines quiver
and speak too, while a cat groans in painful heat.

The wine of your calling burns the nose first, then tongue, throat.
The bone of your calling slipped from an angel who asked
difficult questions of your skin.
(It was saying yes.)
You were told you would never die, that it would be
unnecessary.
The robins were called God's birds since they ate nothing.
Remember?
They fell from your hands and flew into the folds of the wind.
The book opened more, like a pomegranate,
bloody bursts and the grit of seed.

PILGRIMS

We are not sorry
for the waterfall that drowned you, your eyes
cut out and served
on a plate to a despot, not for the cave
or the wheel, your
way to heaven.

We are not sorry for the
clothes we sew you from the sofa-cushion extras,
the rickrack
to adorn your hems, for the black
pennies we leave in a cup at your feet,
and the medallions of what ails us—a pair of ears,
a leg, an evil sprite—pinned to every
inch of cloth.

We are a little sorry for the time we painted you
in the blue and orange
of the Mets—but hey, we all need
benediction. Warmer nights,

up the one hundred steps,
we, the weary, climb
holding tight to the railings, sweat drips
alms into our coffee cups
with blue sketches of the Parthenon

around and around them,
and we begin to ask questions

we are sorry for
later: *How could you*
pray for more pain? Why didn't you
just kill yourself?
Look at us, was it worth it?

TESTAMENT

The cat wants to be a strong thing, a hand, a tree.
The girl wants to be a pirate in a tree.
The tree wants to be the pond with its face of shining.
The pond wants to be the sun that dumps its sugar on the grass.
The grass wants to be the foot, its sole, its heel.
The foot wants to be the brain who always gets to choose.
The brain wants to be the feet dumb in their shoes.
The shoe wants to be the buckle that the girl shines with a cloth.
The buckle wants to be the magpie lifting what shines.
The magpie wants to be the egg in the nest touching its brother.
The egg wants to be the feather.
The feather wants to be the mite, devouring its plume.

SUMMERTIME

Every day we hate you
and every day we give up.
This is the universe's sad persistence.
The Bermuda grass has
laid itself down,
yellow and thin, and
the refrigerator is a hum
so consistent it's
nothing. Did we think
this could be a life? This
thick arctic of heat? This tundra
of struggle? Even dogs
know it's best
to pretend they are dead.

By afternoon we don't
believe in anything:
electrons, snowflakes,
surgeries on the heart—
all idiotic and overreaching.
On couches, under trees,
in cars at the longer red lights, we
succumb, slip off
the way rings fall from
the fingers of the wasting,

and then we wake, lead
pooled in our limbs,
clothes damp and swaddling.

After raw suppers
and booze over ice, when the
stars pretend they are cold,
when we can again bear it,
we hold hands.

The seam of skin on skin
leaks a briny dream.
It is a tiny piece
of whales and wind,
of great boats
that trust gravity every night
to tell them on which blackness
we might float.

YOU WILL COME TO ME ACROSS THE DESERT

I went looking for you,
here of all places.

I said when I get a hold of you,
you better watch out.
You'll never eat sugar
as long as I live and breathe.
I said I will love you more
than there are bats in Carlsbad.
I said don't forget the sunscreen.

I said that if you hurt yourself
I will hurt myself too.
I said OK where are you?
Tell me if I'm getting close,
such as *warm, warmer.*

I said I will love
your small body, your big one. I said
there are some bodies
that can save us.

I said look, a bite of tender skin, a freckle.
I am ready to be saved.
And don't forget a hat and long sleeves.

I said being a widow is not shameful.
I said *parasol* means with or against the sun.
I once had a sister who died

and here the bells of the church ring regularly somewhere
between 6:30 and 7.
I said if I died now, I would die full of regret.
I wish this knowledge did not make me weep.
I said I have found everybody
else—where are you?
Don't step there! The cacti are dangerous.
Trust me, you could die.
I said Jill could show us all about how
to live in kindness, and the sky is
bigger than when we crossed the ocean.

I said symphony of low-riders.
I said you will not be in trouble if
you come home now.

I said olly olly in free.

GRAVID

Who has a hand made of three
lengths of bone? Who has a spine?
A bright bow, a tight string
of shells, white or
whiter?

Who has a kidney and then
another one? Whose foot, articulate
and suddenly forward? What
ear? What four
chambers scattering mountains
across the screen?

Whose right eye shines
a ring of lens through the murk
of skull? Who has a brain?
A long nose? Another ear,
that slim moon in profile?

Whose moon of a home, so plain
you could call it empty, but no.
No trees, no kitchen, books
or clothes. The nothing that everybody has,
or had, or maybe only the lucky.
The nothing

but a working mouth,
and thank you for the other foot,
the other hand.

MIDNIGHT IN THE HOUSE

Tubs of margarine stud the table,
and insects have given up their racecars.
The dishes are
rimmed with a chipped swag of gold.
I had a lot of ideas,
but they became unlinear or not especially
productive or forward-
looking—too many frying pans,

smoky ceilings, sticky red aprons,
the sink that bosses, *Throw the bones out!*
and a painting of Jesus that ignores.
I watch the mother spider in the corner
stroke the hairs of her scabby victim
beyond the edge of sleep.

Why not another song about the pain of love?
Why not another moon, that golden onion
rising acute above our fields?
So and So's grandfather next door

snaps to, wearing accordion and moustache.
His syntactical fingers bully the keys
until actual words from the soul of love

appear to me, as sung by a sweating man
with silver buttons:
love of my love,
and *I am not a sailor,*
and *you who know of life,*
of life between the cups.

THIS WORLD AND THAT ONE

Sometimes you defy it,
I am not that, watching a stranger
cry like a dog when she thinks she's alone
at the kitchen window, hands forgotten
under the running tap.
The curtains blow out, flap the other side of the sill.
In you one hole fills another,
stacked like cups.
You remember your hands.

AFTER THE FIRST ROAD

the next is a habit. It makes hope the way
morning unsullies those still
drowned in their beds, the way a wren

of a word then another gives itself to sentence.
But it's not the dear sock
alone on the dresser, those gladioli larval

in spring or all the other things unbaffling,
home. Surely I must know grief flocks
to any surface, those in motion as well:

the slipper of wind, electric lines diving and
rising, the smooth pates of fields,
and the moon punctuating *Oh,*

After the first road, I admit I'm no longer
going home. To keep from the next,
from the rapt syntax of go, to stop

gorging on the gorgeous, royal unknown,
quit the addiction of the clean slate,
I must try harder.

AFTER

Touching,
touching, not
buying. Like a
snail on a stick,
you, slow over
it with your tiny
mouth, never
biting. Spiral:
the eye,
the head, the repetition
of *help*—omen
turns
omenless. Things—
soft, hard, book,
milk, grass
in the drive, dove
and all—things.
The holy is
otherwise,
nowhere. Where
the not-fog
waits in the
no-cleft.

TWO YEARS IN THAT CITY

It was pouring rain and I went
to the Sunday movie, the title lost to me now,
    at the college cinema with dull vinyl curtains,
    sticky floors, and little tables
to pull out of the arms of your seat,
and, afterward, wandering from the dark
    flickering credits, we all were caught
    in sheets and sheets of rain, shining
tar and shining gothic buildings in a
New England city with stragglers hiding
    in doorways, others running
    with their useless umbrellas towards cars,
the trees themselves heavy and leaning
with that cold bleary fatigue of rain, black
    and gray as the movie itself, where
    Freud and Kafka, wearing intricate suits
and speaking in English about desire
or its lack, the one idea I carried with me,
    the idea I worried like a sore tooth,
    to the parking lot, to the car and when I hit
a jagged thing submerged in a puddle,
what I thought was only a glaze of water
    on the tar and not a hole that hid
    something sharp that tore,
and even through the drum of rain
on steel, on tar, on rooftops, on leaves,

I heard the grind of rim
        on pavement and I stalled.
By then the lot was empty and there were
no phones, so I decided to walk home, why not
        since wet was wet and the car was fine
        for the night, so I walked, sometimes
running because I was cold, through
the neighborhood where no one wanted me,
        the houses on Dart Street with slack
        porches and gutters stopped with
garbage and Freud in his dark suit,
or was it Kafka, kept whispering
        melancholia wasn't the sadness
        of a lost lover, or a city, or a life, but
when you realized you mourned
the glittering, ravenous void of desire itself.

ONCE

I had one foot and one ear and one eye
and no trouble choosing,
let's say, between the blue
and the green.
My God was delicious,
like a fish with no bones.
But somewhere, I

was tired, somewhere
I paced the riverbank
in dry clothes. I was often waiting
for night, waiting for the heat
to slip to other
longitudes, and finally

I found the rope
that would guide me
into the slurry of griefs
in the stomach of the world.
I saw you there.

Sometimes I have a few drinks to forget.
Sometimes I watch NASCAR.
Images are quite useful,
though unimportant
in the long run. Standing in the heat

of the plaza, I eat fried dough.
And give pocket change
to Indians. I promised
that I would
change this time, and then
a plaster Virgin cried
real, bloody tears.

PSALM TO WHOEVER IS RESPONSIBLE

What tiny ears—the size of seashells or the fossils
of seashells. At times I would like to whisper into one or the other
why didn't you finish what you started?
but instead, I say something like
what ears!

Your mouth is everything,
a wedding cake with tiers of flowers
made of spun sugar, labial, thick with butter,
both vanilla and chocolate.
I would eat it but
it's clearly yours.

Your hand is a manila folder; it's a John Henry
and his hammer. It's a smack on a new baby
or new leather chair.
Each finger is a chairperson, a metronome,
or a rule. Your nails are
shields for battle, tablets for commands.

Your will is big as a cruise ship—replete with
buffets, crooners and dancers, casino
and clowns. Such lovely tonnage needs no reason,
slices the face of the Atlantic while above
its starry brow weeps. I wake to the
Panama Canal grinding.

Its gears
drain and fill, drain and fill.

Your idea of the beautiful is slick
and skids under like a hoof in mud or a hotel
at night on a street that can be found
nowhere on the only map.
Oh, mulberry in the yard, gnarled
toes belonging to my neighbor, shopping cart in the river!

And of course night comes on
just as you desired. As do the wild pigs
snuffling in the desert, as do the wolves
spangled with hunger, and the hunger itself
that lopes through my home.
Your desire is dark,
whoever you are, and igneously
formed by heat.
Cooling, it litters my slopes.

A WORLD'S TOO LITTLE FOR THY TENT, A GRAVE TOO BIG FOR ME

There aren't enough doves
in North America to fill
the gondola of you.
Onions are fallible, only
pretending to be infinite,
and the Great Plains—
well, they're not that great.
You might fit a thousand of me
in your purse; the distance
between my nose and lip is mere
centimeters. I know I am only a pat
of butter, a blueberry, an aspirin,
a quivering cell about to dissolve,
to you.

Haven't you noticed that even
the sphinx is growing smaller
each day? What can that fawn,
retreating, legs a pile of cutlery,
expect from the approaching dog?
What good is my will when your voice
is what I mistake the freight trains
that shake my windows for?

When I close my eyes, I return
to the tomb of night. I return
to you, or the idea of you, and
I walk down corridors dragging
my fingers along the wall,
looking for that café, warm
and brightly lit, where I stopped
asking so many questions.
I ate a sandwich and was called
something dear by a stranger.

AMBIDEXTROUS

The right hand says *no problem—help yourself.*
The left hand is never seen eating.

The right hand is tall.
The left hand is short.

The left hand goes for rides with men.
The right hand does like a cocktail.

The right hand checks email, writes about Harold Pinter, his fascination
with the abject, so many hobos and trashcan scenery,
but *the vacuum is a little loud, later?*
While the cord lashes itself back into its hole, the left hand
remembers its ex, swinging at the policeman, and the phonebook falling
into the dishwater.

The right hand in the daytime says *ask the dry cleaner …*
and at night the left hand, shawled with streetlight, uses cheap cell phones
to call people in another country.

The right hand feels angry when the car is towed for sloppy parking,
therefore the left hand is really not going to mention that the rake broke
when it was left in the driveway.

The left hand gets some tattoos.
The right hand refrains from saying this seems inappropriate.

The left hand tries to forget it used to eat peanut butter
with a spoon in the aisles then return the jar to the shelf, and
meanwhile, the right hand can't stop thinking about its marriage,
its fears for its children, the way its arms have gotten scaly with age,
the perpetual ugliness of feet, the neighbor's lousy pit bull.

The right hand at Christmas will give the left hand its old car,
and the left hand will buy the right
some lovely video games where you can build a house
and go shopping.

The right hand reads an instruction manual thoroughly,
while the left hand's heart breaks at the sight of the red gladioli
out the kitchen window.

The left hand loves bath time with the right hand's children.
Afterward, the right hand will kiss them goodnight.

The right hands over wages.
The left hand says *thank you*.

The right hand worries about the holes
in the ozone and the left goes to faith healers.

The left wants to go back to where its mother lives
and the right hand would say, if it spoke about these things, *but I need you.*
The left hand would pretend it didn't hear.

PRAYER OF THE ST. OF THE HOTTEST NIGHT
IN LAS CRUCES

This country has no refrigerator left open but yours.
No ice cube–filled dishtowel but yours.
No parched lawn but this one.

This country sits
on no mended lawn chairs but yours,
exhausted by the golden chin of the summer moon,
the bright mole of Venus. Yours

are the country's flip-flops,
made of rubber pink and white,
stuck between the country's perspiring toes.
Yours is the Bondo-body Tercel
wobbling up and down the strip,
windows open to cool your laps
as you and this country cruise.

This country has no other Guns N' Roses
on the radio but yours, no other White Snake.
Believe me,
no other Colonel Sanders's suit and moustache
glows a red and white signage against the desert night
but yours, and yours
are the dumpsters out back, one for grease
and one for everything else, to which
this country lugs its tender sacks of waste.

Yours is the only meander home,
and yours the television's blue
inside of which this country will cocoon,
sleepy and oblivious to the world,
to smack its lips in a dream.
This country wakes to turn off the light,
and it's no other dark but yours.

TO THE CRICKETS WHICH SING IN UNISON

Crickets saw their wings in the grass at night
    invisible in the yard the push and draw keening
        the moon a bare white
the paring light
the liquid streetlight and dome
    of the bank tumbles off
        the distant rotunda glowing internal
self-feeding
        the push and draw breathing
its light tonight shines through my outstretched hand
    bones there ball and socket end to end
        lock to key the desert city cooling
and silent teeming
        invisible in the yard
sprinklers hiss turrets rise from the grass machine
    undone or doing drag the glowing head
        of cigarette gone against the concrete step
all sparks burn out
        the paring light
down beside me on the still warm stair
    underneath meanwhile a fretworks of plumbing
        crickets saw their wings
breathing
            a desert city cools

UBI SUNT QUI ANTE NOS FUERUNT?

Where are they? The big-nosed ones, the ones
with thin hair who walked with serious faces
towards me. The pale girl who wanted
nothing, the Indian boy who wanted me,

who caught all girls and put them in jail.
There's the teacher in her fur, she rings
the bell, and there's her baby Angelo who never
breathed. There's a hole in the day, one

about as big as a dove, and there are fig trees
and feathers from the dove the cat ate.
There's a skin of green on the birdbath
and a swarm of black flies returning

to the garbage at the curb. Where
is the one who fell under, who trusted me
to sing her home? Where is the cream
of horizon, the snug passage, the arms of night?

Where did my arms go? Where did my skin?
The way I, unashamed and bare, leaned back
against piles of pillows? The beetle with red wings
I couldn't walk without crushing everywhere?

There is the woman who brings me food
on Sundays and the sweat that sticks me
to the chair. Gone is the boat that will cross
me over and here is my house of bones.

RIP

First we'll do away with the waist.
We know you loved the knuckle
of hip, the nothing stem
of waist, but, sorry,
its obsolescence was built-in.

Then, we'll do away
with the nicknames, silly and regional;
anyone still living is embarrassed.
We did away with the brother,
dead since the war, and we'll do away with
the upside down tomato plant
by not watering it—there are more
important things to do.

We'll do away
with the job, then
the cruises, that brocade jacket you put on
when feeling fancy.
We'll do away with feeling fancy.

We'll do away with the car. That
one might hurt a little.
We'll do away with hair,
and your feet will go toe by toe until
the inevitable difficulty emerges,

humiliating you
for a while.

Then we'll do away with
shame and we'll do
away with privacy—what need have you?
We'll do away with dramas and thrillers. Comedies only
to move the days which become nights
or vice versa or what day is it?
We'll do away with your own bed,
your bladder, your eyes.

Last, we'll do away with that dog
because you liked it
much more than we did.

THE ALTAR BY GEORGE HERBERT

Tulips panted against the wall. *So much need to feed*
a crisp stem, I thought, as we put our fingers
in the bullet holes above the bed. Typed captions translated
photos of Rivera, Kahlo, Trotsky and his wife

in her boxy suit, devoted smile, that hopeful hat
with bent feather below an image of the assassin
who would get her husband in the end. George Herbert was
what I translated, *The Temple,* the only book I brought,

where he says the heart must be a stone on which
to build God's altar—no love without affliction:
my hard heart meets in this frame. In those days,
I loved the jungle, spread like wool below

an unsteady sky, and the crumbling pyramid's altar-top
flocked with moonlight. I loved the monkeys
throwing sticks and rinds at tourists from their nests
in the trees. The noise at night, the hysterical crush

of insect limbs rubbing, animal want, all night banged
against the window, each with an urgent song of *me me me.*
How loud the fecund world can be. *Mi corazon duro,*
I wrote, bored, and smoke rose from other tables,

from the wheels of the cars on the cobbled roads,
and once I saw a mouse, suicidal, enter the frantic
crowd. I cried out at the park in Mexico City
where Indians, ropes on their ankles, dove like

fatal birds to the ground while a Hassid, in his 19th century
cloak kept after me, *Speak English? English?* He said,
*We've all become vegetarians. There isn't a butcher
for miles.* I watched his black hat disappear

into the swarm of vendors, masked dancers. Was that it,
devotion? Young and gorgeous for it, I crept away
one night, met a German hippie, and he pulled my swimsuit
aside in the volcanic lake. The fat Costa Rican's coffee plantation

unfolded below, the ranging packs of filthy dogs, the water
so hot and sulfured I gleamed like something ephemeral.
Sometimes I saw movies, cheap Hong Kong action films
dubbed into Spanish with Mandarin subtitles. But that started

to get difficult, the young men dying with extravagance,
the improbable ballet of whizzing swords, gun fights
in teahouses filled with caged birds. Herbert,
consumptive and small country parish-bound,

wrote that struggle must be the same as resolution,
as faith itself, while he suffocated in his sad minister's bed,
for years arguing with God and himself. It's the uglier
business, willing yourself from despair to belief.

In those days, I thought the saints, robes heavy with must,
with ancient, gnarled hands, deserved the nothing
they felt their way towards. In those days, my favorite saints
were the ones who burned away young—I admired them

in the cathedral paintings, hooded eyes, the brutal
wings of their ribs, gilt halos, baroque frames. What does it mean,
devotion? Mothers weep in the corners of those paintings
while a man, each morning, sweeps the church floor.

SPANISH LANGUAGE IN MEXICO, 1993

Klaus, the dreadlocked German welder, tells us
about the swastikas he's seen all over Mexico—saw
them in the resort town, and some men
at the cockfights had them
tattooed on their hands. Klaus reaches over
(narrow nose, smooth chest), spills the granulated Nescafé

into his palm. He licks it, says, *I think they are very racist
here*, gesturing with the jar over the edge of our hotel
roof, to pastel Colonial buildings, the narrow cobbled streets
coughing with buses, newspaper vendors,
and *Indigenas* on blankets selling bracelets,

sweaters, candy, and dolls. The junkie from
England bears a palimpsest of symbols
on his back—roses over tigers over Celtic
swirls and bands—his skin and eyes gone golden
from hepatitis. *My piss is brown* he announced
after dinner last week

while I watched him bathe his needle
with flame. This morning he eyes
Klaus' beautiful wristwatch, handmade boots,
my Grundig short wave. The songs on the radio
at night are melancholic, manic all day.

I find Spanish untranslatable in song,
I say, and men shout up the newspaper's
name *Commercio, Commercio,* while others set up tables
on the road, hundreds of tiny washers, springs,
and screws scavenged from other blenders splayed
on cloth. *Like Indians with their buffalo,* Courtney,
the medical student, says. She sits down
across from me, underlining in a book.
Her language school Spanish lessons are funny,

she continues, where Miguel and Maria
discuss fashion, food, and geography. She repeats some
of the phrases to Klaus who is filling
my cup with more hot milk. My tutor
preaches to me, slips
into my lessons a fresh evangelism of destruction

and peril, makes me uncomfortable
even now, years later,
as I remember his plump, flushed face.
The dangerous time is coming—he almost sang it—
when governments will be one and the citizens of the earth
will get all they desire, a barcode of 666
tattooed on the nape of every neck.
The Bible has foretold. The Nescafé crystals
swirl into my milk, speckling

the surface then releasing their shapes
to my ringing spoon, and I'm riding a horse
with an old silver saddle and sword,

its shoes on the stones
shower sparks on the skeletal dogs which
pendulum these roads. The blond

hair on Klaus's arm as he pours
milk, more milk, has become a refrain for memory,
becomes the gold
of the sunlight in Mexico
in 1993, becomes the warm skin
of a horse. He snorts after lighting
another inexpensive Marlboro,
punches me on the shoulder
with his fist. *So quiet,* he says.
What are you? An intellectual?

IN THE SHADE

Imagine the gnarled bouquet,
the veiny tangle of birds and branch under which you'll sit
as long as you want. Cool your dogs, your forehead,
your wife

where a brim
will succor you and all water stays chill.
The spiders will spit their webby traps
and wait

for flies to stop
giving up, for the cool to juice them
one last time. There will be umbrella,
metal

shed, the building's
afternoon dark twin of shadow,
and they will soothe. Soon someone will beat the air
with a fan,

and a stretching cat
will ooze one perfect yawn. Who won't be cooler?
Who will not be more thankful and easy-going?
Soon there'll be water

and watching dust motes
fume just outside the lip of sun.
The swallows will offer up song, swing,
and mud.

Imagine mud
and mulch, think of crotch and womb,
think of breath and eyelids closed. Think of snow. Pray
the cactus,

spiny hugger,
will not interfere. You've been walking all day.
Remember, no matter how hard you tried,
there were no proper

shoes for this. Think
of the long porch at your grandmother's,
think of cement unscored by sun.
Don't worry, soon

shade will come.
You'll exhale, grow paler, drift past
desire, your thirst becoming an abstraction. Then
sweat

will live only to chill
your shirt to your breasts and the crown
of your hat will be clean. Dry hands and small of
back. Soon.

UNFINISHED LETTER TO DEATH

Sorry to bother you, especially in this time of

Though we've often passed on airplanes, at the library, in the desert, I've never

I am writing to you, heart heavy with the pain of

First allow me to introduce my colleagues and their

Let's be honest: that dog had already

And we really didn't know that bacteria

In the ring, most boxers

Vodka itself is not so terrible if

The tobacco industry has systematically

You see, if I had only been ten minutes earlier,

The toaster and the hairdryer are indeed flawed appliances,

It only took one despot, a painting by Degas, and an angry mistress to

War, to many of us here in the United States, wastes

Please, think of the

How much would it take to

From now on, I will

This is to advise you that you are not to come within

Without further adieu,

THE SELF AFTER MODERNISM

The poem I write next will be better. This one starts
in a hopeful manner, but soon feels lost

or thin. True, I have been prodigal, wandered
through foreign lands, and I have spent all my money

on silly things I should not have
(a purse with cats on it, terrible Mexican candies, an ancient blue

station wagon, a permanent wave), but
I swear this poem will be better,

though historically
I am quite lazy and won't wash my face

unless I have to. I do not sweep under the bed
and would eat pastry everyday if there was a good

bakery. I say I'll write a better poem, even though
this afternoon, a gregarious spring day

bounding across the park, over the swing set,
gazebo and into

my windows, I lie on the couch,
unable to believe in anything except

potential—the poem should have a looseness
that lately I admire, language that, nonetheless,

draws blood, and a range beyond the personal
foibles of its maker. The poem I will write

won't have a
middle section that gets flabby.

I feel responsible for it, the poem I will write,
which I can imagine with ultrasound clarity,

something fierce and kicking in the darkness.
Watch the poem swing its little arms, open its mouth

to a vast, fetal silence.
For motivation,

I listen to a recorded lecture on Surrealism,
which tells me I am a constant

collage, a brilliant and ever-changing work in progress.
(For what else is the Self after Modernism?)

I am a furry teacup, a cello riding a bus,
yes and no meeting on a street corner

in Paris, incongruous or binary!
Maybe there's some hope for this poem

if I open the door to the random, the fragmented,
the flimsy scraps that more genuinely

compose the day, the mind, the night, the dream.
All the crazy little pieces

that will never make sense, never climb off the couch,
press a shirt, comb their hair,

walk out of the house and get things done.
But who doesn't want their poem to be better

than they are? I have been waiting a long time
to write this poem, which, as of yet,

is not to be trusted. And where is that penetrating
ending, when all accumulated
grief and humor
now shivers, slick and wailing,
ready to judge the world?

NOTES

Some of these titles were borrowed from or echo titles of poems by Adam Zagajewski.

"As Well As You Can" began with a Mark Wunderlich poem, "Poem Beginning with a Line by Cavafy," which borrows a line from the Cavafy poem, "A Young Poet in His Twenty-Fourth Year."

"The Internal State of Texas" follows through on the idea presented by a bumper sticker that "Texas Is a State of Mind." Esequiel Hernández was an American shot by a US Marine on an anti-drug operation near the Mexican border in Redford, Texas, in 1997. He was tending goats.

"What Is True Is You're Not Here" mentions the southwestern tradition of *descansos*, roadside shrines to those killed in car crashes, usually at the location of the crash.

"I admit that I believe ideas exist regardless" is a quotation from George Boas's *The History of Ideas*. The phrase "house of bone" was borrowed from Sheila Black.

"Annunciation" comments on a detail in many images of the annunciation, where Mary is depicted as reading a book when she is called by God to be the mother of Jesus.

The title "A world's too little for thy tent, a grave too big for me" is from the poem "The Temper (I)," by George Herbert.

"Prayer of the St. of the Hottest Night in Las Cruces" takes its form from a prayer, "Christ Has No Body," attributed to Teresa of Ávila.

"Ubi sunt qui ante nos fuerunt?" is Latin for "where are those who were before us?" It is also a form of poetry that meditates on death and transience. This poem echoes a section of "The Wanderer," collected in the Exeter Book.

"The Self after Modernism" contains references to a lecture presented during a Warren Wilson MFA residency. Any errors in representation are mine. Also, many thanks to "Ch'vil Schreiben a Poem auf Yiddish," by Jacqueline Osherow.

CPSIA information can be obtained
at www.ICGtesting.com
Printed in the USA
LVHW041101090419
613496LV00001B/152